TEDDINGTON, KINGSTON & TWICKENHAM
AN ILLUSTRATED WALK

GARTH GROOMBRIDGE

AMBERLEY

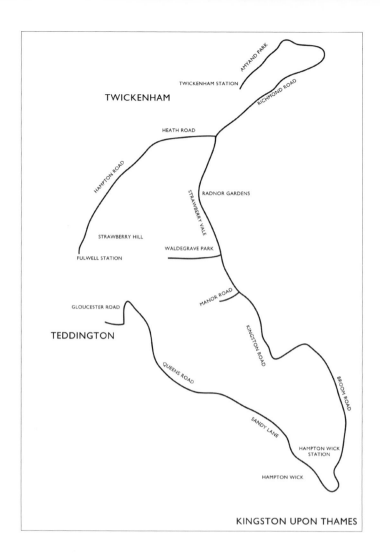

TWICKENHAM

AMYAND PARK

TWICKENHAM STATION

RICHMOND ROAD

HEATH ROAD

HAMPTON ROAD

RADNOR GARDENS

STRAWBERRY VALE

STRAWBERRY HILL

WALDEGRAVE PARK

FULWELL STATION

MANOR ROAD

GLOUCESTER ROAD

TEDDINGTON

KINGSTON ROAD

QUEENS ROAD

BROOM ROAD

SANDY LANE

HAMPTON WICK STATION

HAMPTON WICK

KINGSTON UPON THAMES

First published 2013

Amberley Publishing
The Hill, Stroud
Gloucestershire, GL5 4EP

www.amberley-books.com

Copyright © Garth Groombridge, 2013

The right of Garth Groombridge to be identified
as the Author of this work has been asserted in
accordance with the Copyrights, Designs and
Patents Act 1988.

ISBN 978 1 4456 1610 0 (PRINT)
ISBN 978 1 4456 1625 4 (EBOOK)

British Library Cataloguing in Publication Data.
A catalogue record for this book is available from
the British Library.

Typeset in 9.5pt on 12pt Celeste.
Typesetting by Amberley Publishing.
Printed in the UK.

Introduction

The thinking and format of this book is not quite the conventional one. I've always been interested in architecture, and have over the years photographed old or interesting buildings – in particular where I used to live: the Teddington, Hampton and Twickenham area of the former county of Middlesex. Most of those photographs, taken from 1970 until the early 1980s when I moved away, were in the form of colour transparencies, but it was only in 2006 that I first considered the possibility that they might be of interest to others. Rather to my surprise it seems that no one had yet extended the 'past and present' comparison format to the 1970s, while local historians had often all but exhausted their trove of Victorian and Edwardian, or 'between the wars' collections. So my first book in 2007, *Teddington, Twickenham & the Hamptons: Past & Present*, recorded a period at the very edge of another wave of urban change – the big houses still being systematically demolished, many of the small shops destined to vanish (often converted into residential use), churches closing down; landmarks threatened.

My next book, *The Changing Face of Richmond, Petersham & Ham*, followed in 2008, and a more comprehensive book, *The Changing Face of London Since the 1970s*, has finally been published in 2012. However, together with photographs taken while researching the earlier book, there still remained a number of 1970s pictures for the Teddington, Twickenham and Kingston upon Thames area, and it is some of these, together with more recent photographs taken between 2006 and 2012, that now comprise this book.

However, instead of the conventional 'then and now' approach, I wish to take the reader on an imaginary 'walk', exploring and celebrating the local vernacular architecture, starting at Hampton Road, Teddington, and exploring a few of the Teddington backstreets, before briefly crossing over the River Thames to Kingston upon Thames, then back to Hampton Wick and through riverside Teddington to Twickenham, where we will venture as far as St Margarets, before finishing at Hampton Road, Twickenham. On the way there *will* be comparative glimpses of the 1970s (or occasionally earlier), but at other times we will merely view the area's rich architectural heritage through the eyes of the present, the often-ignored or unnoticed everyday houses from the last 300 years, right up to the more interesting and attractive post-modern style.

Some might object to Kingston being included in a book featuring Teddington and Twickenham. The argument being that Kingston is in Surrey – indeed it was once regarded as the county town before that status officially moved to Guildford with Kingston's inclusion within the GLC area – while Teddington, Twickenham and Hampton Wick were in the old county of Middlesex, north of the river, formerly (after 1937) part of the borough of Twickenham; later (after 1965) the borough of Richmond upon Thames. It is tempting perhaps to slant our view of history by these often rather arbitrary, official boundaries, created (more often than not) by some thoughtless bureaucrat; yet for most ordinary people such divisions – between one town and another, between one municipal borough and another, even one county and another – had little relevance.

While some local historians, and even publishers, might protest at the inclusion of Kingston, for most of the late nineteenth century and the first half of the twentieth century Kingston was the birth/marriage/death registration office for Teddington and Hampton. Even as a child living in Teddington in the 1950s, it was to Kingston we often went for serious shopping, rather than Richmond, Hounslow or more distant Staines. So from a local viewpoint our excursion across the river into Kingston would have been quite normal. Remember too, that for hundreds of years from the twelfth century onward (until the 1729 Fulham/Putney Bridge, Westminster Bridge in 1750, and bridges at Kew, Blackfriars, Richmond and Battersea in the second half of the eighteenth century) Kingston was the only Thames road crossing above London Bridge. Until the first Hampton Court Bridge was built in 1752–53, the next bridge west was at Staines. The small linear village of Hampton Wick probably owed its very existence to Kingston Bridge.

Geography (notably the Thames) and history have combined to make this one of the most interesting outlying districts of London. If nothing else, the purpose of this book is to show that away from the tourist hot spots of Hampton Court Palace, Marble Hill House or Syon House there exists a hidden but equally fascinating heritage.

Garth Groombridge

Teddington

PART I: HAMPTON ROAD TO SANDY LANE

As a child living at various times in both Teddington and Hampton Hill, I had fond memories of Hampton Road, with its eclectic mixture of large (mostly Victorian) villas strung out along the north side, from King's Road to the junction with Stanley Road; and the later – more modest – middle-class, twentieth-century, detached houses, often constructed where there had once been agricultural land, orchards or gravel pits. On the south side were two – seemingly secret – accesses into Bushy Park, from what are now Blandford Road and Laurel Road. Pictured above in 2007, one such large Victorian house in Hampton Road, on the corner of Anlaby Road, is listed in the 1911 edition of *Kelly's Street Directory* as 'Hampton House'. The portrait photograph to the right, taken some time in the early 1970s, shows the original, more ornate, roofline.

'An Englishman's home is his castle', and obviously Edwardian-period building developers took this quite literally, as can be seen here in Gloucester Road, with this delightful castellation to what would otherwise be a comparatively ordinary suburban semi-detached home. The photograph was taken in 2011.

One of the often-neglected joys of vernacular architecture is the sheer variety of style; this again is in Gloucester Road (this is No. 7, seen in 2007), but with its lofty stepped gable it almost has a hint of Scottish baronial.

Emerging from Gloucester Road into Stanley Road, although the Elms and the Old Hollies have gone, at least some of the larger late Victorian houses have, as yet, survived. No. 66 (photograph taken in 2007) on the corner of Somerset Road is the first of four large houses, now all long since divided into flats, between here and Sutherland Grove (then just a cul-de-sac), listed in the 1911 *Kelly's Directory* as Somerset House, Bolton Lodge, Stanley House, and The Limes. As a child in the 1950s I lived with my uncle and maternal grandmother in a post-war prefab halfway along Somerset Road, near what is now Stuart Close, which cut through from Sunderland Grove around 1960. In 2012 this property was being refurbished.

Above and middle: Two photographs taken in 2008 of the early nineteenth-century assortment of houses, Nos 1–47 Queens Road, between the former Queen public house on the corner facing onto the junction with Broad Street (closed in the 1950s, now a laundry), and Little Queens Road. Most were apparently always residential, although the 1911 *Kelly's Directory* listed No. 3 as a 'wardrobe dealer', No. 5 as a laundry, No. 7 as a 'watchmaker', and No. 35 as a 'general store'. The 1953 *Kelly's* still listed No. 5 as 'the Boot & Shoe Hospital' and No. 7 as 'Frank H. Stride & Son, House Furnishing'.

Below: Taken in 2008, this is a hidden part of Teddington, Nos 1–2 Park Street, with the old Mission Hall beyond – a rare gravelled and unsurfaced cul-de-sac, off Queens Road, almost opposite Little Queens Road. Again the 1911 *Kelly's Directory* listed No. 2 as 'Ellington Villa', while the Mission Hall (built around 1883/84) was the 'London City Mission Hall'.

Opposite: Just past Park Street is Coleshill Road, an L-shaped road of late Victorian and Edwardian (mostly semi-detached) houses connecting Queens Road back to Hampton Road. From here, in turn, a short (apparently unnamed) road connects to one of the pedestrian entrances to Bushy Park. On the 1894 Ordnance Survey map there is no sign of this access (although the entrances to Blandford Road, and what has since become Laurel Road, are marked). Instead, the main Teddington access to Bushy Park would appear to have been in Queens Road, opposite Park Lane, through what is now one of the entrances to the National Physical Laboratory. The NPL was established at Teddington in 1902, initially occupying Bushy House and soon extending east along Queens Road and to the south of Coleshill Road; eventually, of course, it extended as far as Teddington Hall and Hampton Road. It therefore would seem that this essential pedestrian access into Bushy Park may have been opened as a compromise, given that the next entrance is in Park Road. Later, however, as the NPL spread westward along the internal newly laid-out Kelvin and Rayleigh Avenues, I suspect they came to regret having this public right of way cutting across their territory, but by then there was nothing they could do about it. This building, photographed in around 1969/70, although constructed sometime in the 1930s (and marked on a 1973 NPL site plan as 'RAD SC') was located almost opposite the Rayleigh Gate. The mid-1950s saw the next phase of post-war expansion, in particular the construction of two very modern concrete-and-glass buildings – the six-storey Charles Babbage Building between Kelvin Avenue and Stanton Avenue, and the four-storey Sir Neville (or Nevill) Mott Building, next to (and connected with) this older building. Three floors of this building actually extended right across the roadway, and so immediately above where I stood when I took this photograph. The eastern end (which would have been on my left) was supported on two massive concrete pillars. At the time of construction they were probably the most 'futuristic' buildings in Teddington! As near as possible the same view, taken in 2012, and all of the above mentioned buildings were demolished in 2010. The pedestrian gate to Bushy Park can just be seen in the distance.

Above: Thankfully the still-delightful backstreets between Park Road and Teddington railway station are part of the greater Park Road conservation area (first set up in 1974, extended 1980). In the photograph above, taken in the 1970s, we see No. 5 Albert Road, also known as Alma Cottage, a listed mid-Victorian stucco villa which still looks much the same now.

Again off Park Road, just down from Albert Road is Clarence Road, and here we see the old Wesleyan Methodist chapel (also known as Craig Hall) built around 1859, although dated on the pediment as 1860. Within twenty years the congregation was such that a new chapel was built at the junction of Stanley Road and Hampton Road to replace it, where the triangle of green is now, and this building was subsequently used by the Baptists. In its later incarnations it was a courthouse and used by a local playgroup, but has now been converted to residential use. Properties in Clarence Road date from 1853 onwards, while those of Albert Road – later apparently designated as 'Station Gardens estate' – were being laid out around 1879. With the extension of the line from Hampton Wick to Richmond, nearby Teddington railway station was opened in 1863.

The former Clarence Hotel, Park Road, seen in this photograph from 2007 as viewed from Park Lane, has been perhaps rather needlessly renamed the Park, when it changed ownership and was renovated in 1996. Although this Grade II listed building – which one internet commentator likened to a railway station – only dates from 1863, there has been an inn on or near this site since 1730. It was originally named the Greyhound Inn, and later renamed the North Arms in 1790, when Lord North's wife was Ranger in Bushy Park; then five years later it was renamed again as the Guildford Arms. Finally, it was renamed after the Duke of Clarence, later King William IV, when he assumed the rangership, living as he did in Bushy Park House. Still a hotel, it boasts forty-three rooms and the Park Café Bar restaurant.

Seen here in 2011, Nos 26–28 The Causeway, located between The Causeway and Middle Lane, viewed from Park Road – now with a dental surgery on the ground floor with apartments above. It is an excellent example of post-modern elegance, almost perfectly matching the two eighteenth-century detached houses, Clarence House and Adelaide House (Nos 14 and 16), located just to the left, out of the picture. This was once the site of Teddington's long-lost town hall (which included a ballroom and theatre), built in 1886 and burnt down in 1903. It was never rebuilt. In the 1960s a car showroom and garage for AV Motors stood here until it was closed in 1984.

The distinctive Lloyds Bank building at No. 23 Teddington High Street, which, apart from the trees now planted in front, looks almost no different from an earlier photograph I took as long ago as 1971. At that time the main Teddington post office was just out of the picture on the left, on the corner of Elmfield Avenue, while Guy Salmon's motor repair garage was a few doors further along on the right. This delightful building was purpose built as a bank in 1931, designed in 1929 by the Arts and Crafts architect Albert Randall Wells (1877–1942) at the request of John (Montie) Pearse, then chairman of Lloyds Bank, for whom Wells had already undertaken work at Pearse's home, Wardington Manor.

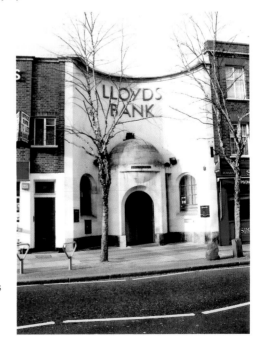

This photograph, taken in the mid-1970s, would now be almost impossible to identify apart from the sign on the extreme left-hand side of the building. This shows the name (in part) of Guy Salmon, whose motor repair shop in the High Street once occupied what is now the rather bland Troon Court, between the former post office (still Royal Mail) and Vicarage Road. Returning in 2012, I was unable to see any surviving identifiable structure. All of the area at the rear of what had been Guy Salmon's is now Cairngorm Close. Note, however, the buildings on the right, with the wooden weatherboarding; we shall see other (this time surviving) examples later.

Opposite above: No. 109 Park Road (also known as Bushy Park Cottage), on the corner just down from the junction with Queens Road, can be seen in this photograph, which was taken in the late 1970s. Hedges and other shrubbery have since then partly obscured the view. According to research by local historian P. A. Ching, the oldest part of this property dates to around 1745, with a Victorian period wing added around 100 years later, sometime before 1863. There is a Regency veranda leading to the rear garden. Park Road was widened in the 1920s, sadly necessitating the felling of many trees along the east side.

Opposite below: Immediately next door, still in Park Road (just), but facing the entrance to Bushy Park and Chestnut Avenue, is another delightful property; once the entrance lodge to the former Bushy Lodge, a large extensive property that occupied much of the site south of Clarence Road, where Avenue Gardens now is. Bushy Lodge was sold off in three lots in 1915 and the house itself was eventually demolished in 1928. In the 1915 sale brochure the entrance lodge was listed as containing a 'sitting room, two bedrooms, a kitchen/scullery, WC, wood shed and coal cellar'. This photograph was taken in 2006.

One of the mostly late Victorian/Edwardian houses along the north side of Sandy Lane, between the entrance to Chestnut Avenue and the 1851 gasworks next to Bushy Park Road. The inset photograph was taken sometime during the 1970s from Bushy Park. Upon returning here in 2011, unfortunately much that has been built since the 1970s is architecturally bland and uninspired, and I could not identify this house as having survived. Hidden behind Bushy Park's high brick walls is a shamefully neglected piece of almost-forgotten Teddington history – that of the 60-acre Camp Griffiss (codename Widewing), the USAF base established in July 1942 and named after Lt Colonel Townsend Griffiss. Griffiss was apparently the first US airman to die in Europe in the Second World War, shot down by friendly fire. Initially used by the US 8th Air Force from March 1944 until December 1944, it became General Eisenhower's Supreme Headquarters for the Allied Expeditionary Force (SHAEF), and it was from here that the D-Day landings (Operation Overlord) were planned. Against the advice of some of his senior staff officers, Eisenhower actually preferred this location 15 miles from the centre of London. During this period anti-aircraft guns were deployed in the Royal Park. The Leg of Mutton and Heron Ponds, as well as the Diane Fountain, were drained and covered with camouflage netting. In its heyday 1,600 US personnel and almost 1,300 British were stationed at the camp. Briefly used by the RAF after the war, it was closed in 1952 and the remaining buildings (by then merely concrete shells) were finally demolished in 1963. Now, apart from the bland 1960s Sheaf Way housing estate off Sandy Lane, and the pedestrian Sheaf Gate, there exist only a few, rather unobtrusive memorials dotted about the site. Above, the larger photograph taken in 2011 is that dedicated by the RAF to the USAF, the inscription of which is only easily readable by climbing over the low railings that surround it!

Hampton Wick & Kingston

SANDY LANE TO KINGSTON BRIDGE, MARKET & RIVERSIDE

Strangely the Teddington and Hampton Wick parish border zigzags back and forth across Sandy Lane until Bushy Park Road, next to the old gasworks, itself now gone and the site being massively redeveloped into new blocks of flats. Just past Vicarage Road and Thatched Cottage, the road name reverts back to Park Road, but this time in Hampton Wick. Ingram House, a good example of a 1930s-style block of flats, can be seen here undergoing renovation in 2011, built on the site of the former parsonage or vicarage.

Inset: Still in Park Road, Hampton Wick, and a view taken in the 1970s of the Old Cottages, Nos 52–68. They dated to around 1700, and a black-and-white 1911 photograph of them with metal railings along the street frontage can be seen in the Hampton Wick section of Mike Cherry, Ken Howe and John Sheaf's 1996 *Britain in Old Photographs: Twickenham, Teddington & Hampton.* An enquiry letter, dated 1963, concerning their age and history remarks that 'one has two wells, one in the kitchen, covered over' apparently supplying 'sweet water within inches of the surface', while the other well was 'outside the back door'. Which cottage this was is not stated.

This and previous page: Two further photographs of cottages in Park Road, taken around 1970–71. It is interesting to note they were built on long, narrow plots of land, presumably extending as allotments at the rear. However, upon returning in 2011 (*above*) the former openness has gone, and instead trees and shrubs have now almost completely concealed the view from the road. Privacy for the owner/occupiers has been gained, but once again (as I have remarked in my previous books) this is a loss for us amateur historians.

Inset, a 1970s view of Home Park Terrace, Hampton Court Road, with those nearest to the entrance to Hampton Court Park (or the Home Park) dating from the eighteenth century. From left to right: Fern Glen; The Gate House (dark brick, steps up front); Home Park House. The Kingston Gate Lodge is beyond the building with the low roofline, on the far right. The 700 acres (280 hectares) of Home Park extends all the way to the gardens of Hampton Court Palace, and has been open to the public since 1894. The main picture shows Home Park Terrace as seen in 2012.

The above picture (actually taken of the parked vintage sports convertible with its bonnet open) is looking towards Kingston Bridge. This was the replacement for the old twelfth-century bridge opened in 1828, and was designed by local architect and Hampton Wick resident Edward Lapidge (1779–1860), who also designed a number of local churches – St Mary's, Hampton; St Andrew's, Ham; and St John's at Hampton Wick.

These photographs, taken in around 1970–71, show the archaeological excavations of riverside Kingston, and the site of the medieval bridge just to the north of the modern nineteenth-century bridge. Of special interest is the jumble of almost exclusively commercial businesses on the Hampton Wick side of the river, which in the later view, taken in 2008, has completely vanished. This is now almost entirely residential, luxury apartments. A part of the medieval bridge and a building undercroft (dated *c.* 1350), originally located beneath the old Rose and Crown Inn at the north end of Old Bridge Street, were subsequently encased in a concrete tray and removed from the site in 1986, and two years later relocated to the basement of the John Lewis store.

Inset, a photograph taken in 1971 of the westerly end of Clarence Street looking towards Kingston Bridge (seen on the left – the nearest tree is actually on the Surrey side). The junction with the northern end of Thames Street can be seen on the left, leading towards Horse Fair, with Old Bridge Street extending behind the Edwardian mock-Tudor building. By the middle of the nineteenth century, time and neglect had reduced the ancient medieval and Tudor houses between Wood Street, Lane Water, Thames Street and Horsefair to unsanitary slums. Eventually (following the 1888 Kingston Improvement Act) all 'the old buildings and their undesirable inhabitants' in the immediate vicinity of Horse Fair and the northern end of Thames Street were cleared away by 1905, only for their modern early twentieth-century replacements to be similarly demolished just over eighty years later. The larger picture is as near as is possible to the same view seen in 2008, with the John Lewis underpass (now re-designated as Horse Fair) diverting traffic away from the old town centre. The bridge was widened in 1914, and again in 1999–2001 to four lanes. Some maps rather bizarrely extend the name Horse Fair to include the A308 road as it crosses the bridge itself.

It is now almost impossible to replicate this 1971 view of the north side of Thames Street and Horse Fair (*inset*), seen from the Clarence Street junction, with Old Bridge Street out of sight but off to the left. Leon Costumers is on the right, with the attractive red-brick-and-stone façade of the South East Gas Board showrooms beyond. Instead, the 2008 view above is of Clarence Street looking towards the bridge; All Saints' church is out of the picture to the left. Wood Street is seen here leading off to right, with the Bentall Centre (the former Bentalls department store) out of view to the right of this picture. The massive (some may say intrusive) John Lewis/Waitrose complex (almost twenty-five years in the planning, eventually opened in 1990) now occupies the entire former network of old streets between the riverfront and Wood Street, dominating both the view and entrance to Kingston from the Middlesex side.

It was in 1867 that Frank Bentall first opened his drapery store in Clarence Street, and by 1935 they had expanded to dominate the retail end of Kingston. They then commissioned the huge and very impressive Wood Street façade, designed by architect Aston Webb in the Sir Christopher Wren 'Hampton Court Palace' style, with stonework by Eric Gill. Throughout the rest of the twentieth century, whenever the opportunity arose, Bentalls purchased land adjacent to the core Kingston site, enabling further extensions to be systemically added, including one into Fife Road in 1964. Indeed, from 1935 to 1976 they were reputed to be the largest department store in the UK outside of central London.

In 1947 they opened their first branch store in Worthing, followed by (among others) stores in Ealing (1950), Tunbridge Wells (1960) and Bracknell (1973). The Worthing and Tonbridge stores are now part of the Beales group.

In 1987 Frank Bentall's great-grandson, Leonard Edward Bentall, instigated the massive £130-million redevelopment scheme to incorporate the Bentalls store into the ambitious Bentall Centre, a giant new 600,000-square-foot retail complex with over 100 shops and food outlets, facing onto a vast five-level central atrium covered by a 100-foot-high barrel-vaulted glass roof. In addition, over 1,200 exclusive parking spaces were to be located on the west side of Wood Street, connected by a high-level covered pedestrian bridge. The famous Wood Street into Clarence Street Aston Webb façade was retained and successfully integrated into the new design, while – as seen in the 2008 photograph opposite above – a new entrance opened onto a now pedestrianised Clarence Street. The other three pictures on this spread give a glimpse of the interior, again in 2008, with the last two (*above*) taken in 1992, the year the project was completed. Since 2001 the Kingston and Bracknell Bentalls stores have been owned by the Yorkshire-based, family-owned Fenwick Group.

The lower end of Thames Street viewed from Market Place, seen inset in 1971, when the central building (Nos 3–5) with its 1902 Dutch-fronted façade was then occupied by the British Home Stores (now known, of course, as BHS, having since moved to Eden Walk). Before that it was Nuthall's restaurant and function rooms, an old established Kingston firm of caterers dating back to the early half of the nineteenth century. In 1980 it had become the camping equipment store Millets, seen here in 2008. For much of the twentieth century Boots the Chemist had occupied the two buildings glimpsed on the right of the 2008 photograph, Nos 14–15 Market Place. The corner building dates to 1590, while the tall façade of its neighbour is Edwardian, designed between 1909 and 1928, and depicts important people connected with Kingston, including King Edward the Elder, Saxon King Athelstan, King John, King Edward III and Queen Elizabeth I. From the second half of the nineteenth century until 1908, Phillipson & Son's private subscription lending library was located at No. 15, listed in the 1895 *Kelly's Directory* as 'George Phillipson, printer, bookseller & stamp distributor'. No. 14 was 'E. Nuthall & Sons, tobacconists'. Boots moved to Eden Walk in the 1980s, and in 2008 Nos 15–16 were a Next store, but on my latest visit in 2012 it had changed ownership again, and become Jack Wills, University Outfitters.

Inset, another 1970s view of the Market Place, this time facing in the opposite direction towards the junction with Church Street. The south entrance to All Saints' church is on the nearside left. Although there was a church here in Saxon times, nothing of that foundation has survived. The base of the existing tower is thirteenth century, while the upper portion is Georgian, from 1708, and further restoration work during the Victorian period obliterated anything medieval. A map from the seventeenth century suggested that at one stage the market extended still further north on either side of the church, joining up with Horse Fair. Church Street itself was once a pig market, while the trading of other livestock in the Market Place apparently stopped in the 1920s, 'after an incident with a sheep in Boots the Chemists' (quoted from Tim Everson's introduction, *Alan Godfrey Maps*, London sheet 140). Livestock was then moved to Fairfield, where it was eventually discontinued shortly after the Second World War. Above is the same view in 2008; more pedestrian-friendly certainly, with trees and flowers, but the downside perhaps is that, with all the neat and trendy French and German food stalls, a certain shabby but endearing vitality to the market itself has been lost.

Another 1970s view of the junction with Church Street, viewed from the east side of Market Place, and again below in 2008. The more recent picture aptly illustrates the total lack of any apparent architectural harmony displayed when the tall, narrow building at No. 22 Market Place – at one time K's Shoes, now occupied by the hairdressing chain Toni & Guy – was inserted between the two older structures sometime in the 1960s. Typically, it would seem, no effort was made to integrate style, material, windows, floor level or even roofline. For many years No. 22 was a public house – as the King's Head dating back to 1636, after 1835 The Greyhound, then after 1857 The Mitre, and finally by 1891 The Criterion. It closed in 1910. Later in the twentieth century it was Newman's Ironmongers. Below, the same view in 2008.

A 1970s view of the funnel-shaped Apple Market, leading off the southern end of Eden Street, with the narrow entrance to Crown Passage glimpsed on the left. This was formerly named Harrow Passage after the Harrow public house, which closed in 1912. Like the now-vanished Horse Fair, the Apple Market dates from before 1500, indicating that even by that time the main Market Place was becoming too small to carry out all its functions.

There is little of architectural interest on the right-hand side, and the old Morning Star public house on the corner of Eden Street is now an O'Neill's. The mixture of 'real' communal shops and small businesses (such as the butcher and radio repair shop in the older picture, and the saddler, florist, ironmonger, leather merchant, hosier and bookmaker listed in the 1928 *Kelly's Directory*) has given way to a twenty-first-century pizza takeaway; the Studio Hairdressings; The Terrace (No. 6a) with its smart middle-class clientele seated outside; Food For Thought, and a beauty parlour; Beauty by Honey. No. 9, on the corner of Crown Passage, is still (both in 1928 and as I always remember it throughout the 1950s, '60s and '70s) a bakery, now Stiles.

Two views – both from the 1970s – of the then Griffin Hotel, No. 1 Market Place, viewed from Eden Street, with Clattern Place and the Hogsmill Bridge leading away on the left into the High Street. Certainly a public house and coaching inn since the middle of the sixteenth century, and sometimes known as the Golden Griffin, in the nineteenth century it had strong Tory connections. By 1934 it was owned by the Hodgson Brewery, but in 1985/86 it was sold and converted into the Griffin Centre, comprising shops and a restaurant, although the frontage with its golden griffin emblem and royal coat of arms has been preserved. In 2012 the street façade is dominated by Laura Ashley and yet another barbers, Hair Masters. Out of the pictures, to the right, No. 3 Market Place is still the Druid's Head hotel. The clock seen in the first picture still reads the 'Kingston Building Society', but in 2012 was occupied by the Royal Fish Bar ('Traditional English Fish & Chips').

Two photographs of the old post office at the junction of Ashdown Road and Brook Street (on the right) viewed from Eden Street. The first picture was taken in the 1970s, while the second was in 2008, showing the ground-floor windows boarded up. A Grade II listed building, it was originally built in 1875 on the site of the old Surrey Militia barracks, and was closed (despite much protest) in 1997. In 2000 while being used by Kingston University's art department it was vandalised following a rave party. At the time of writing in 2012, the building is still closed following the developer Hammerson pulling out of the K+20 town centre project in 2007. There is now a community campaign to reinstate the post office here, moving it from the existing location in the Eden Street shopping complex.

As demolition approaches, a glimpse of one of the narrow pedestrian passageways leading off Young's Buildings Passage, looking towards Eden Street, sometime in the 1970s. For so long the heart of medieval Kingston, by the 1980s commercialism and the motor car meant that all of this part of Eden Street was to be swept away; alas, only to be replaced by the usual bland, unimaginative walkways and ugly, almost claustrophobic architecture of Eden Walk. A triumph for consumerism, but, I suspect, rather disheartening visually and for the human spirit, and probably (even as seen below on a sunny day in 2012) a place better to avoid late at night. Such was progress as we mindlessly hollowed out our ancient town centres in readiness for the twenty-first century. Primark's store can be glimpsed in Eden Street.

This photograph, again taken in 1971 (although from the almost empty streets and closed shops presumably on a Sunday), shows the junction of the north side of Clarence Street with Fife Road. On the left can be seen the rather plain 1930s Art Deco Clarence Street façade of Bentalls department store immediately opposite Church Street. With the opening of the newly aligned Kingston Bridge, Clarence Street (originally called Norbiton Road) was extended westward from London Road, sweeping away the eighteenth-century houses around the churchyard, to give Kingston a more modern east–west shopping axis. It was named after the Duchess of Clarence, later Queen Adelaide, wife to William IV, who had opened the new bridge in July 1828.

In the same view, taken in 2008, what is now the Bentall Centre was completely transformed in the late 1980s, while Clarence Street, between Wood Street and Eden Street, is now pedestrianised – a vast improvement to the traffic-congested 1970s, where shoppers literally took their lives in their hands every time they attempted to cross the busy road.

A 1970s view of Clarence Street, just past the junction with London Road, Eden Street and Fairfield Way, viewed from what was then the front façade of the C&A store (1956–96), now Wilkinson's. As can be seen here with this mock-Tudor frontage, even then the town's Edwardian-period commercial architecture was often more eclectic then attractive. Returning in 2012 this jumble of contrasting styles has itself been swept away and replaced by two-storey blandness, but perhaps more appropriate to the kind of commercial premises seen here. What has survived, however, is the former Kingston Empire Theatre (Nos 153–57 Clarence Street, aka the 'New Empire'). The theatre was originally built in 1910 by Bertie Crewe, although its interior was completely gutted in 1956 when it ceased being a theatre and was converted into offices and a supermarket. Since the 1990s the ground floor and half of the first floor has been a large Wetherspoon's pub/restaurant, now called The King's Tun, but the rest of the building is owned by London Church International, with church offices and conference rooms.

Delightfully shabby and unplanned back in the 1970s, and still not yet tarted up even now, in 2012, this is the older, north side of the Old London Road, just down from the former C&A (now Wilkinson's) department store, and the junction with Clarence Street. Once this was the main road into Kingston from the east, but it is now blocked off to traffic at the Clarence Street junction. David Mach's playful urban artwork of domino-like red telephone boxes, entitled *Out of Order* (1988), now dominates the main pedestrian roadway. Immediately opposite is the old Victorian police station (now the 'Kopshop'), with the date 1864 over the entrance. Seen here in the distance of the older picture are the Grade II listed Cleaves Almshouses (twelve two-storey dwellings, Nos 49–71 London Road), built in 1668 on land bequeathed by William Cleaves, a liveryman of the Haberdashers Company.

Emerging from Kingston railway station in the 1970s, this is the view one would have had, with the junction of Wood Street and Fife Road on the right and the Clarence Road/Cromwell Road junction on the far left. Dominating the view is the elegant 200-foot frontage of the Victorian Italianate Kingston Hotel and public house, from 1869. When it opened it boasted a 30-foot by 18-foot refreshment room, coffee room, tap room, parlour and bar parlour, and another large club or dining room upstairs, together with a billiard room and fifteen bedrooms. Modernised in 1932–33, with a snack bar and two dining rooms, it was the headquarters of the Kingston Wednesday Football Club, and the Kingstonian Football Club from 1934. A Watney Combe pub, the landlord from 1909 to 1951 was William Smurthwaite. It closed soon after and was partly used as the head office for John Perring Furniture and partly occupied by the Westminster Wine Co. In 1964 it was a grill bar and restaurant, seating 120.

Back in 2008 and, apart from the buildings in Fife Road, everything else has been swept away in the 1980s as part of the ring road scheme, leaving a rather dreary urban landscape, and, indeed, one which could be almost anywhere. The old 1922 bus garage in Clarence Street (which I remember as a dark, gloomy, cavernous place, almost like an aircraft hangar, where passengers felt like intruders) has gone and a new bus interchange is now in Cromwell Road. The new Rotunda complex occupies the Clarence Street site, comprising a fourteen-screen Odeon multiplex, tenpin bowling, restaurants and leisure club, with the distinctive old Bentalls furniture depository building still visible from Cromwell Road.

This and next page: Leaving Kingston, we cross back over the bridge to Middlesex, and here we see above and on the following pages the contrasting views of the Kingston riverfront, taken in the 1970s and then in 2007, with the previous pictures showing the once clearly visible tower of All Saints' parish church and the rear of buildings in Thames Street – now almost completely obscured by the later, post-1980s redevelopment.

This and next page: Although the 1970s photographs of the Kingston riverfront as seen from the Middlesex bank opposite are not a complete panoramic view, nevertheless they capture something of what would have then been seen as you walked south from the bridge along the Middlesex towpath. However, starting in the 1980s, and continuing into the early 2000s, almost the entire Kingston riverfront has been completely redeveloped, from the railway bridge and Water Lane to the north of Kingston Bridge, stretching south, past where the Hogsmill river flowed out into the Thames, and on to where the High Street becomes the A307 Portsmouth Road in the south. Look at these photographs and decide for yourself if what is there now is an improvement on what was before. It was a jumble of boathouses and slipways; mostly inaccessible river frontage; old, often rather tumbled-down properties – although, admittedly most of the older buildings actually facing onto the High Street *have* survived, although 'tidied up'. It still reflected something of Kingston's history and medieval origins. The new buildings from the 1980s onward – mostly luxury apartments or catering outlets – could have been transplanted from anywhere: the London Docklands, Bristol or Cardiff Docks, Reading, or Baltimore, USA. Such is change.

Right and below: The east side of Hampton Wick High Street and the junction with Old Bridge Street, looking north, seen in the early 1970s and again in 2012. Old Bridge Street originally aligned with its now obliterated namesake on the Surrey/Kingston side of the river, marking the ancient medieval crossing point. As we have seen above, until at least the 1970s the riverbank here comprised of wharfs and timber sheds south of the railway bridge, before giving way to grander residential riverside housing along Lower Teddington Road.

A view of the east side of Hampton Wick High Street in the early 1970s (*inset*) and one of 2012, where, for the most part, the properties are now better maintained, but often lacking in that vitality of purpose our high streets once had. Although a very ancient settlement, dating from Anglo-Saxon times at least, Hampton Wick has always been constrained by its geographical boundaries: the Thames and Hampton Court to the east and south, Bushy Park and Teddington to the west and north. Civic independence as an Urban District Council was brief, from 1895 until absorbed into the borough of Twickenham in 1937. Like its neighbour Teddington, the west side of the High Street was demolished in 1906 to widen the road for the tramway, but otherwise the street layout is probably much the same as it was in the sixteenth century. In 1962 much of what *had* survived was again threatened by wholesale demolition with the proposal for a bridge flyover which would have effectively wiped out much of the old village. Fortunately concerted local opposition and sanity prevailed, and one long-term consequence was the Hampton Wick Society.

Another early 1970s view (*inset*) showing the junction of Park Road (on the left) with the High Street (leading off in the direction of Upper Teddington Road and the railway station on the right), with St John's Road out of the picture in the left-hand foreground. This is No. 45 High Street. The Foresters public house and former hotel is still there, but now styling itself a 'gastropub', with pavement area extended. More user-friendly no doubt, but something of the architectural clarity of the previous picture has been lost by the planting of the tree.

An interesting 1970s view of No. 60 Hampton Wick High Street, with its distinctive white weatherboarding and two period Mini cars out front; one stands on a concrete inspection ramp, as it was still a motor repair garage then. Even as long ago as 1934 *Kelly's Directory* already listed it as being 'Grove Motor & Engineering Works', while what were obviously the former workshops, located in the yard behind the main house, are now advertised as possible offices or warehouse space, with roller steel shutter doors. The junction to Seymour Road is out of the picture to the left.

Seen again in 2012, this is now Navigator House, a Grade II listed building divided into offices. The sign says 'Serviced office suites available from £60 per week'. Occupants include an architect, landscape gardeners, and the Jeevika Trust, a charity set up to address rural poverty in India. One internet story relates that it was built in the eighteenth century by a navigator who saw similar buildings in New England – hence the name. However, such weatherboard buildings were once comparatively common, not only in Kent and Essex, but also Middlesex – we have already seen other such examples behind Teddington High Street, and will again later in this book, in First Cross Road and May Road, Twickenham.

Teddington

PART II: FAIRFAX ROAD & KINGSTON ROAD TO BROOM ROAD & TWICKENHAM ROAD

Returning to Teddington, and crossing to the other side of the Teddington to Hampton Wick railway line as Station Road turns away east, becoming Cromwell Road, Fairfax Road continues on running parallel. Formerly it had a number of large detached houses with big gardens that were once so characteristic of the area. Looking at both the 1894–96 Ordnance Survey map and the 1925 *Kelly's Street Directory* gives a glimpse of these – now mostly lost – properties, listing Crossway, Vernon Lodge, Lincoln House, Kingswear, Meadow Bank, Ellerslie, Fairlea, and Brookfield. These, some of the earliest of my photographs, were taken in 1968/69, and show the demolition of one such large house located at the Cornwell Road end of Fairfax Road. In this instance part of the site is now occupied by Grosvenor Court, seen on the following page in 2011.

Above: The original 1969 prospectus by agents J. & A. Offer & Partners for Grosvenor Court (see previous page) describes it as comprising forty-two flats (with quite spacious, well-planned interiors), of one, two and three bedrooms, set in landscaped gardens, with a 1,000-year lease. Of course, many such large houses were being acquired by local developers and demolished at this time.

Opposite above: Buried deep in what are now the West London suburbs, it is often forgotten that as recently as the first half of the twentieth century much of this area of Teddington was still predominately agricultural and rural. In 1900 the population of Teddington was just 14,000. Above is a view from 2011 of what is now No. 44 Cromwell Road, opposite the junction with Kingston Lane. On the 1894 Ordnance Survey map there are only five large houses shown on this (the south) side of Cromwell Road, while to the left and behind this house, was an 'Udney Farm'. Again in the 1925 *Kelly's Directory* this may have been Udney Place.

Opposite below: Immediately opposite the last photograph of Cromwell Road is Kingston Lane, running back towards Teddington High Street with a number of delightful large, detached, early Edwardian-period houses. In the 1911 *Kelly's Directory* they are listed as No. 71 Kernah, No. 69 Macequece, No. 67 Meadow View (now called Wisteria House), No. 65 Invencargill, No. 63 Chez Nous (seen here), No. 61 Riverholme and No. 59 Heathwaite. We will soon see more examples of those ornate Edwardian white wooden balconies and fancy porches on the other side of Kingston Road, in Broom Road and King Edward's Grove especially.

Emerging into Kingston Road and turning in the direction of Teddington Lock, we come to Nos 112–14, seen in the 1970s (*inset*) and above and below in 2012, probably dating from the pre-First World War late Edwardian period, and only really made that much more interesting than other properties hereabouts by the delightful, almost American-style, wooden verandas. Again a profusion of trees and shrubbery have made their frontages less obvious to the passer-by, but the survival of such architectural eccentricity is all the more charming to those that seek it out.

This page and above on next page: Located between Nos 17 and 21 Broom Road in the 1953 *Kelly's Street Directory* is The Anchorage, actually on the corner of Broom Road and Broom Water, seen above sometime in the 1970s, and again in a 2007 photograph with apparently very little changed apart from the modern cars! Already on the 1894–96 OS map the narrow creek from the Thames situated behind this property had been lengthened by a speculative late Victorian builder named Charles Drake, who subsequently, from 1899 onwards, developed the Broom Water estate – although it was originally called Hambledon Road. However, by 1907 Mr Drake was bankrupt, and further housing continued piecemeal between then and 1915, and again from 1930 until 1965. A large house, The Trowlock, was formerly located where the 1960s-period townhouses now are. A 1988 sales brochure describes The Anchorage as 'backing onto Broom Water' (Drake's long narrow channel extending from the Thames almost to Broom Road itself), and having its own 30-foot mooring and refurbished boathouse, while the house itself comprised a drawing room, dining room, study, kitchen/breakfast room, conservatory, master bedroom with en suite, five other bedrooms, bathroom and a 65-foot garden.

On the 1894–96 OS map of the Teddington Lock area there were only three roads linking Kingston Road with Broom Road between what is now Broom Water and Trowlock Way – Holmesdale Road, Munster Road and Cornelius Road. Of these only Holmesdale Road had a random smattering of early housing development. Cornelius Road was later to be patriotically renamed as King Edward's Grove (after King Edward VII, although interestingly No. 59 is still named as 'Cornelius'), while sometime around the early 1900s, two new roads appeared – Atbara Road and St Winifred's Road. Architecturally most of the houses in Atbara Road are rather ordinary, until No. 106 (*see lower picture, next page*), the last house on the right as you approach Broom Road, which suddenly gives this example of Edwardian exuberance.

This and next page: On the same side, but actually in Broom Road, is No. 90, Burleigh House, which has fascinated me since my childhood, as I walked past to what was then Broom Road Secondary Modern School (now an academy school) in the early 1960s. Built around 1903, this is perhaps the best, and most extravagant, example of this delightful local style of ornate wooden balconies – almost American Colonial in appearance – examples of which we have already briefly glimpsed in Kingston Lane. As we shall see in the following pages, this extended along Broom Road and down King Edward's Grove, with lesser examples in Elmer's Drive, running parallel to Kingston Road. During my 2012 visit to this area, I was offered a glimpse of the interior, which has elaborate stucco bas relief over the doorways, stucco ceilings, an almost manorial hallway/staircase, and possibly an original Arts and Crafts-style fireplace. The current owner and I speculated that perhaps this might have been the building developer's own house. It certainly occupies a prominent position. The first photograph on the next page, taken in 2012, is the Atbara Road frontage; while the picture below, taken in 2011, is viewed from Broom Road.

While Atbara Road comprises rather ordinary early twentieth-century houses, by contrast King Edward's Grove (originally named on the 1896 OS map as Cornelius Road) is almost entirely given over to numerous variations of this fascinating Edwardian style, a mixture perhaps of American Colonial and the Arts and Crafts movement. Whether detached or semi-detached, no two are exactly alike, with their fancy wooden first-floor balconies, porches and verandas – some extremely ornate, with intricate wooden filigree. Others are plainer, but often still have interesting sensual curves, exterior stucco and rendering, while some now sport additional windows in the roof. Here and there can be glimpsed an original front door, but overall even modern replacements (especially white PVC) do not seem completely out of character.

This and next page: Back in Broom Road, and these photographs, taken in 2011/12, show more examples of the same style we have seen in Atbara Road and King Edward's Grove. One problem when trying to find occupants or former house names in otherwise very useful directories like *Kelly's* is that often the house numbers from (for instance) the early twentieth century have been reallocated and changed since. This is particularly so from the 1920s, with extensive building development and infilling. However, when I consulted the 1910 *Kelly's Directory*, the numbers matched from King Edward's Grove proceeding towards and just beyond Atbara Road. The houses were listed as No. 102 The Hey, No. 100 Ravenscroft, No. 94 Harvard Lodge, No. 92 Yale Lodge, No. 90 Burleigh House (the only one, incidentally, still to retain its original name), and No. 88 Atbara Cottage (seen above on next page) on the opposite corner of Atbara Road. While the older houses in Broom Water became part of a council-designated conservation area in 1977, and this was extended in 2003, but only since then was the area extended again to include these properties, most of which were built between 1903 and 1906.

This and next page: Later alterations to road layouts can sometimes bring confusion to the modern motorist or walker. Kingston Road and Broom Road were eventually connected by Ferry Road, which in one direction leads to Teddington Lock, although nothing ever came of the much-needed Thames road bridge – proposed as long ago as the 1930s. Thus it is that, apart from the 1888 footbridge here, and a small ferry boat which used to run from Twickenham's riverside across to Ham Street opposite (revived in the late 1960s, but which ceased operating in 1995), there is no other way to cross back and forth from Middlesex to Surrey between Kingston and Richmond. Ferry Road continues as far as St Mary's church, then becomes Teddington High Street, but Kingston Road ends at the Ferry Road junction and transforms briefly into Manor Road. This originally then curved left, crossing over Twickenham Road, which starts by St Mary's – the old Teddington manor house having been located opposite, behind the houses and shops on the north side of the High Street. The original manor house, where St Alban's Gardens now is, dated to the mid-sixteenth century, but the last manor house, built in 1800, was demolished in 1896. Now Manor Road is sliced in two, the short lower half continuing straight on as Twickenham Road, leaving the upper half of Manor Road and a truncated section of the old Twickenham Road in isolation. Seen above, in a photograph from the early 1970s, and on the next page in 2012, are two delightful Victorian Italianate-style semi-detached houses, now Nos 28–30 Manor Road. In the 1925 *Kelly's Directory*, the occupant of No. 30 is listed as being a solicitor.

This and next pages: Continuing along Twickenham Road, and Grove Gardens on the left marks the once extensive grounds of Teddington Grove, possibly built by the Swedish-born Scottish architect Sir William Chambers (1723–96) in around 1765 for Jewish merchant Moses Franks. This was later (1797–1812) owned by the founder of *The Times*, John Walter. It was demolished in 1923, although the stables can be seen on the corner of Teddington Park Road. The Grove Gardens estate was developed there from between 1925 and 1930, originally by Royal Dutch Shell for their employees. A little further on, half hidden on the left, is Waldegrave Park, a fine example of large late Victorian villas, mostly in the red-brick Queen Anne Revival style, and built in the early 1880s following the death in 1879 of Frances, Countess Waldegrave, widow of the 7th Earl of Waldegrave, whose family had inherited Horace Walpole's estate at Strawberry Hill in 1811. At this time they probably typified the attraction for many incomers to the locality, men and women seeking work as servants, gardeners and domestics – among them my maternal ancestors from as far afield as Suffolk and Abergavenny. Sadly, by the 1970s the building developers were already eyeing up these desirable plots of land, and in 1984 Nos 51, 53 and 55 were all threatened with demolition, prompting 200 local residents signing a petition demanding they be listed. On the following pages can be seen some photographs taken in the 1970s, along with the same (and neighbouring) properties seen in 2012.

Above: Still in Waldegrave Park, Nos 53–55. In 1988, Richmond upon Thames council had prevented a local Hampton Hill builder from illegal demolition of another property.

Right: No. 66 Waldegrave Park, seen here in 2012, was being marketed in 2003 as The Cleal, having six double bedrooms, three bathrooms, a double drawingroom, a kitchen/breakfast room, a family room and a cellar, with a 199-foot-long rear garden. On this, my return visit, I met a contract lady gardener just leaving, and remarked that, 100 years ago, my maternal grandfather may well have been employed here in a similar capacity!

Twickenham Road now ends and continues as Strawberry Vale. Seen here in another early 1970s photograph is Clyde House, No. 109 Strawberry Vale. This was one of a number of large, elegant houses backing onto the river, particularly distinctive with the inverted V-shaped glass cover-way from front door to the ornate street entrance (a similar example can just be glimpsed through the gate on the corner of Somerset Road and Church Road, Teddington). It does not appear on the 1845 parish plan, but a resident is listed from 1865 onward. It is now the headquarters and registered office of the Richmond Fellowship International, a mental health charity.

As the older Victorian and early Edwardian period buildings fade out, most of the post-First World War twentieth-century architecture here is typical of suburbia at its worst – bland, repetitious and rather boring. One exception as we approach Twickenham is No. 51 Strawberry Vale. Like the flats in Park Road, Teddington, it is another interesting and imaginative example of elegant, post-modern, vernacular domestic architecture. It might well feature in the pages of *Ideal Home* or Channel 4's television series *Grand Designs*.

Twickenham

STRAWBERRY HILL TO ST MARGARETS
& BACK TO FULWELL

For me Teddington ends and Twickenham begins where Strawberry Vale becomes Cross Deep at the junction with Waldegrave Road, with Radnor Gardens facing onto the river on the right. Formerly the gardens of the original Cross Deep House, once located where River View and Bonser Road is now, it was acquired by the then Urban District Council in 1902 and opened as a public gardens the following year. For a child in the 1950s and early 1960s this was a magical place: the bowling green on its own island, still divided by a small stream until 1965, while the eighteenth-century Chinese summer house, seen here looking spick and span in 2012, was then delightfully shabby and derelict, hemmed in by the wall and hedges and the open Gothic-style gazebo beyond. The ghostly foundations of Radnor House, bombed in 1940, became an enclosed garden-within-a-garden, while naturally the entrance to Alexander Pope's grotto, like a mysterious but inaccessible cave under the main road, also held a childhood fascination.

Even as late as the 1940s Cross Deep still had a number of grand mansions on either side, mostly from the eighteenth century. On the riverside was Radnor House and Cross Deep Hall, then the Grotto Hotel and later the Pope's Grotto public house, which was destroyed by a V1 in 1944. In the late 1970s it was replaced by the current building and then became a pub-restaurant and hotel, renamed The Alexander Pope. Almost opposite is the Grade II Ryan House seen here, built in 1807 by Sophia Charlotte, Baroness Howe of Langar, who had bought and destroyed Pope's house, which formerly occupied the site. The garden front is one storey lower because of the slope down to the river. Following her death in 1835 the house was partly demolished and divided into two – River Deep and Ryan House, renamed as Castle Ryan in 1907 when it was converted into flats. The other half of Baroness Howe's house was destroyed by a V1 bomb in 1944.

Moving quickly through the congested King Street (which is better covered in the old Victorian and Edwardian images elsewhere) we step into the more tranquil charm of Church Street, once (until York Street was cut through in 1899) the main route east to Richmond. Here a glimpse of an older Twickenham has survived (at least in part), with narrow streets and alleyways leading down to the river, ancient houses, shops, and, at No. 39, what has been known since at least 1769 as The Fox public house. The earliest reference is to a pub called Le Bell, *c.* 1700, although a 1749 court document already states it was 'formerly called the Bell', implying the name had already changed.

Twickenham's prominent if rather forgotten Art Deco building, No. 42 York Street, is located on the corner of Arragon Road and York Street. Once the Electricity Board showroom and offices, it is now part of the Civic Centre used by the Adult and Community Services and Education and Children's Services Directorate. Obviously dating from the 1930s, it still has the original bas relief depicting symbolic light bulbs and rays over the windows, with more fascinating bas relief over the main door. How many passers-by fail to observe the rather oriental faces seen in the first-floor frieze? That said, however, enquiries with local historians as to who was the architect or exact date of construction draw a blank, although Mike Cherry from the Borough of Twickenham Local History Society believes it dates from between 1931 and 1937.

These two pictures, taken in 2011 and 2006 respectively, show where York Street becomes the Richmond Road, viewed from the now pedestrianised top end of Church Street. Everything seen here dates from after York Street was cut through from the King Street/ London Road junction in 1899. Unfortunately not all the attractive Edwardian façades have survived. Seen here is the former billiard rooms (now the Richmond Camber of Commerce, the bas relief over the central lintel having been very effectively erased) on the site of the Lyric cinema, while next door (now the Shell petrol station) was another, larger cinema, the Twickenham Kinema, seating capacity 1,200, and a very impressive façade, which opened in 1928. This later became the Queens in 1940, then (after being used as a furniture store during the Second World War) the Gaumont in 1944, eventually closing in 1956. However, long before that up until the First World War it had been occupied by a carriage works, latterly known as 'Twickenham Motorworks'.

This and next page: As we proceed along Richmond Road there is an interesting mixture of styles and periods – late Victorian public houses like the Royal Oak (back now to its original name after an incarnation as The Twickenham Tup) and the Old Anchor ('a Young's pub since 1897'). There is also Lebanon Court, a large complex of 1930s blocks of flats, stretching away down Sion Road, along with elegant terrace houses and a cluster of small shops and businesses, some hidden away set back from the main road. Like so much of this area, the 1894–96 OS map shows once extensive nurseries (where Lebanon Court is now, for instance) and orchards either side of Crown Road. Then, immediately next to the old Amyand Lane footpath, there is this discreet-but-delightful gem, seen here in photographs taken in 2006 and 2012. Originally known as 'Crown Crescent' (appearing as such on the 1891 census), this was Nos 149–61, a dozen period cottages, both terraced and semi-detached. Some still had the original trellis porches, and beautifully kept front gardens. They were built in the 1840s by two separate developers, the division being the cut-way to several more cottages at the rear.

What is now Orleans Road was part of a large oblong of land originally parcelled out in the 1720s immediately opposite the junction of Crown Road with what eventually (with the opening of Richmond Bridge in 1777, replacing the ferry) became known as Richmond Road. These modest, two-storey cottages in Orleans Road are on the west side, seen here from the car park at the side and rear of the Crown public house in the 1970s and again in 2006. Chapel Road, Montpelier House and Southend House fringed the south side, with Montpelier Road on the east facing Marble Hill Park. More cottages and the local post office once stood where the car park now is.

Two comparatively recent views of the Crown public house, No. 174 Richmond Road, seen here from the junction of Crown Road: one taken in 2006, the other in 2012, when it had been rather insensitively repainted. This was part of the same parcel of land as Orleans Road, dating from the 1720s, although it only appeared on the list of licensed victuallers in 1730; however, it was already called 'The Crowne'. It was a free house until 1950, and was later (around 1960) sold to Whitbreads. Even during the 1960s I remember it was associated with live jazz music, a tradition which apparently still continues with the Richmond & Twickenham Jazz Club, although performances are no longer free; instead there is an admission fee (according to the website, currently about £10–12). In 1980 both interior and exterior underwent renovation, returning it to a more Victorian décor, while in 1985 a French restaurant was opened in the single-storey annex. In 2012 it was again closed while further alterations were being undertaken.

Two views of the former Rising Sun public house, No. 277 Richmond Road, which (rather to my surprise) has been a pub since 1841, the core building actually being listed. In 1972 the then owners, Watney Mann Group, had a restaurant extension built at the cost of £50,000 converting it into a Schooner Steak House, and it is shown in this incarnation in the first photograph. During this renovation the main building interior was 'much altered', while the restaurant (which I remember frequenting on a number of occasions) had a timber-and-stonework interior and a seating capacity for eighty-four patrons. It boasted 'steak, chicken and fish meals at sensible prices, served in comfortable surroundings'. Alas, time moves on, and by 1992 it had become a Beefeater pub/restaurant with 'Dickensian bric-a-brac and Turner paintings'. However, in 1999 Laing Homes proposed the demolition of the restaurant extension to build seventeen flats and nine four-bedroom houses, although their plan to convert the main building into flats did not materialise. Closed for several years, eventually Young's Brewery acquired it in 2001, and in 2003 it was designated the area's 'favourite local', with live 'easy listening' music, as seen in the 2006 photograph.

Finally, returning in 2012, the Rising Sun has bizarrely been renamed The Marble Hill, and is once again up for sale, the latest option being that, after 170 years, it would instead become a Sainsbury's Local store!

Just past the former Rising Sun public house and opposite the Victorian St Stephen's church (consecrated in 1875, although the tower dates from 1907) can be seen another terrace of old, brown brick cottages, Nos 281–93 Richmond Road. These are Selina's Cottages, dated 1831. In the 1935 *Kelly's Directory* Nos 279–81 were listed as 'tea rooms'.

Two early 1970s period photographs of St Stephen's Gardens, which connected Richmond Road with Sandycombe Road. The mostly detached houses look much the same in 2012, almost forty years later. Interestingly, on the 1894–96 Ordnance Survey map, the location of St Stephen's Gardens was marked as a long, seemingly empty space between orchards and greenhouses. Being neither particularly old, nor always especially memorable perhaps, we rather take such houses from this late Victorian/pre-First World War period for granted, and yet almost every house was individual and interesting, the product of some architect or local builder-developer. In a way these houses are as much a part of our heritage as the churches, town halls and grand mansions. Their loss – often demolished to be replaced by bland, dreary, look-alike boxes – is our loss also.

Above: From St Stephen's Gardens we emerge into the older Sandycombe Road, and here, No. 31 on the corner of Claremont Road, is another delightful example of Victorian Italianate, fancy bow-windows, ornate balcony and corner turret. Interestingly the 1939 *Kelly's Directory* lists the occupant as being a builder. Just down from here, opposite, is Sandycombe Lodge, designed and built in 1807 by the artist J. M. W. Turner (1775–1851) who lived there until he sold the property in 1826. Originally called Solus Lodge, and later undergoing alterations, the house was rescued from dereliction in 1947 by Professor Harold Livermore and his wife Ann, who lived there until his death in 2010, after which the property was bequeathed to a trust. Although the front is rather concealed by trees, it is possible to see the commemorative GLC Blue Plaque.

Opposite: Three views of Sandycombe Cottage, No. 79 St Margaret's Road, with Sandycombe Road, first seen above, sometime in the 1970s, then still occupied by Eldridge Builders. Returning in 2008, while I was researching my *The Changing Face of Richmond, Petersham and Ham*, I found it boarded up and derelict, and presumably (so I thought) destined for demolition. However, returning again in 2012, I was pleasantly surprised to find that this distinctive building has survived, and is being converted to residential use (*see inset*).

Above: Photographed in 2012, Victoria Lodge, on the corner of Rosslyn Road and St Margaret's Road, was described in a sales brochure as a 'detached Georgian coach house, built *circa* 1820'. According to the same estate agent's brochure the interior comprised a drawing-room, kitchen, three bedrooms, dining room, bathroom, steam room, and an 'Italian stepped garden at the rear'. Formerly this was one of two lodges (the other was at the other end of Rosslyn Road, where Richmond Road meets St Margaret's Road) which led into the nineteenth-century Twickenham Park estate.

Inset: No. 1, on the corner of Arlington Road, is one of a number of large Victorian houses (most dating from the 1870s and in the Italianate style) in Rosslyn Road. The original Twickenham Park (or Isleworth Park) was founded in 1227, and lay within the boundary of what is now St Margaret's Road and the Thames, once stretching from the River Crane at Isleworth to what was formerly called 'Ferry Lane' in the south. In the medieval period it was used for breeding rabbits and hunting, and one famous resident was Francis Bacon, philosopher and statesman, who lived here at the beginning of the seventeenth century. However, by the 1820s it was being broken up and new villas were built. One of these, St Margaret's House (also known as Kilmorey House) on Kilmorey Road, gave its name to the locality after 1854. This part of the estate was already being sold off and developed as long ago as the 1850s, although the area nearest to the river was only eventually developed after Twickenham Park House was demolished in 1929. While largely hidden from view, these delightful late Victorian houses in Rosslyn, Arlington and Riverdale Roads are a few of their kind to have survived in the borough. In the 1910 *Kelly's Directory* this is listed as 'Carisbrook House'.

Again almost unnoticed behind what is now the car park of the St Margaret public house (the former St Margarets Hotel), and in addition mostly screened by trees and shrubbery, are Park Cottages, a terrace of thirteen working men's 'two-up, two-down' cottages facing onto a pedestrian passage linking Crown Road with St Margaret's Road. Similar cottages, of course, are to be found throughout the borough – we shall see more like them in both First Cross Road and South Road. During the 1960s the author himself lived in one of a terrace of four such early Victorian cottages in Cross Street (formerly Providence Road), in Hampton Hill. They can already been seen on the 1863 Ordnance Survey map, when Crown Road was still called 'Crown Lane'. In the estate agent brochures they constitute a 'charming parade' and the current price per property is just under £500,000!

What is now the commercial and business heart of St Margarets only came into existence from the 1880s onwards, with the opening of the railway station on the then London & South West Railway in 1876 and the subsequent construction of The Broadway parade of shops around the junction of Crown Road and St Margaret's Road, including what was then the St Margaret's Hotel, the rather opulent entrance of which can been in this 2012 photograph, although now it is just the St Margarets public house. The date '1887' can be seen over the post office opposite, while the parade of shops extending north of the railway from Broadway Avenue to Bridge Road has the date '1896'. The 1896 OS map shows huge swathes north of the railway as undeveloped, open space or orchards to London Road and Whitton.

Just over the railway bridge, off St Margaret's Road but on the opposite side to the railway station, is Downe House, Downes Close, originally one of ten large houses collectively known as Ailsa Park Villas. But while in the last 100 years all of the others have been completely swept away (bombed or wantonly demolished), it was supposedly here, at what was then No. 4 Ailsa Park Villas, that Charles Dickens was reputed to have once stayed during the summer of 1838, writing *Oliver Twist* and *Nicholas Nickleby*. I first heard this story back in the early 1970s, when my first wife and I attended a party here, invited by a work colleague, Christopher Tippet. On a website discussing Charles Dickens in Twickenham, Chris's brother Richard (who I also remember) recollects members of the Dickens Society visiting in 1966, but other sources in the Richmond Local Studies Collection dispute this was the actual house. Downes House is now divided into flats.

Inset: Predating even the railway or the 1870s railway station (seen here in 2012) is Amyand Park Road, connecting St Margaret's Road with Arragon Road and London Road. This rather unusual name has its origin in one Claudius Amyand (1680–1740) a French Huguenot 'of St Martin in the Fields', who was Sergeant-Surgeon to King George I, although actually it was his third son Thomas (1728–1762) whose name is commemorated, having married one Francis Rider of Twickenham. However, according to the Twickenham Museum records of the Amyand connection, what would be called Amyand Park Road was formerly called Shoes Lane, and later (more logically perhaps) Isleworth Lane. The 1863 OS map showed it looking quite rural, unnamed and almost devoid of buildings.

Continue along Amyand Park Road, past what is now the Reformed Evangelical Baptist chapel (originally founded in 1889 and rebuilt in 1952), and a footbridge across the railway marks where Turk's Lane (later Turk's Road and now Winchester Road) once cut beneath the railway to join Amyand Park Road. Here, where the road abruptly turns away from the railway, you can see (in the 1970s photograph, inset) what was once a typical parade of mixed commercial and residential working-class properties, but which (as they do not appear on the 1896 Ordnance Survey map) must date to the turn of the twentieth century. The junction with the older, late Victorian Beaconsfield Road can be seen in the right-hand distance, from which a much older footpath (in 1896 named as Amyand Lane) ran out across orchards and nursery land to Richmond Road (the lower half is now Marble Hill Gardens). In 2012, the single-storey commercial premises on the left is No. 148, the French Connection Garage, motor repairs, while the former shops have now been all converted to residential only, now Nos 142–46 Amyand Park Road. Only the end building has the original brickwork.

Continuing down Amyand Park Road, between Greville Close and Victoria Road, are a number of large, even rather grand, Victorian, mostly semi-detached houses with front porticos and steps, and two storeys above a basement floor – now of course universally sub-divided into flats, as seen here in 2012. Some properties have been linked by what some see as an ugly, intrusive fire-escape; insensitive perhaps, but then our ancestors were often concerned with practicality over beauty.

At the junction of Amyand Park Road and Oak Lane is the rather unassuming Devoncroft House (aka Devoncroft Lodge); its rough-cast stucco appearance belies its age and history. There has been a property on this site since at least 1635, while by 1722 in a bill of sale it was referred to as 'Gardiner's House', and later, between 1840 and 1863, Grove Cottage. However, by 1894 it was already divided as Devoncroft House (which faces onto Oak Lane) and Grove Cottage (facing Amyand Park Road, out of the picture on the right). It has been a Grade II listed building since 1986.

A mystery solved! When, in 2006, I was researching my first book featuring my 1970s photographs, this was one of these photographs whose exact location evaded me. Even at the time I thought it was probably taken from the London Road railway bridge, looking towards Grosvenor Road, but it was only when researching this book that I eventually found confirmation, in the 1969 *GPO Telephone Directory*. Tile Decoration (Sales) Ltd, telephone number 01 892 5272, was listed as at 4 Railway Approach, while the Driving Centre (Twickenham) Ltd, telephone 01 892 2256, was opposite at 5a Railway Approach. Nothing in this photograph has survived, all being swept away in 1977 for some rather ordinary-looking townhouses, seen below.

This is now the Clifden Centre, viewed from Clifden Road, having become part of the Richmond Adult College in 1982, and the Adult & Community College ten years later. This photograph was taken in 2007. This was originally the Twickenham County School, opened in May 1909 with ninety pupils and six staff under headmistress Miss Ethel M. Roberts. The motto was *Summa Petimus* – 'We seek the highest'. By 1923 there were 350 girls and 20 staff, and a new wing was added in 1936 with the number of pupils increasing again, to 495. It had fifteen classrooms, a central hall, art room, library, chemical laboratory, gymnasium and domestic room, and took girls from ages eleven to fourteen. The grammar school fees were only abolished in 1974 when it became a comprehensive, the name changing from Twickenham County Grammar School to Twickenham Girls' School. By 1958 it had 850 girls, but eventually in 1978 a merger was proposed, and in 1980 – not without controversy – it was finally closed and combined with Kneller Girls' School. This is still a fine example of Edwardian civic architecture, from a time when such buildings, whether schools, town halls or railway stations, didn't all look the same: dreary, grey, anonymous boxes.

Again taken in 2007, a view from almost immediately opposite: the broad junction where the tree-lined Clifden Road now meets Copthall Gardens, a delightful example of a large Victorian Italianate semi-detached villa.

This and next two pages: Just over 100 years ago Heath Road between Holly Road and Lion Road was mostly still comprised of large houses or nursery land. Obviously very soon into the twentieth century this more rural landscape between Twickenham town itself and the next urban cluster around The Green was developed, and the last surviving house from this period, Clifden House (on the corner of Clifden Road), was demolished as recently as 1974. Nowadays Heath Road (appropriately named as the road once leading to Hounslow Heath) is a busy, bustling place, with parades of three-storey Edwardian shops, large commercial premises, including a timber yard, and new, post-1980s period blocks of flats. Above and continued over the following pages are photographs taken of the various floats and vehicles seen in the 1981 Twickenham Festival, with (except for the last picture) glimpses of Heath Gardens and The Dip seen in the background.

This last picture, featuring the 1981 class of the Lady Eleanor Holles School (actually located in Hampton Hill) is taken from the Heath Gardens side of Heath Road, looking across to the parade of shops between Lion Road and Laurel Avenue. As always, when looking at the young, eager faces, I cannot help wondering, thirty-plus years on, where are they now?

A sad sight! Even into the twenty-first century Teddington and Twickenham had a number of small, long-established family businesses that had survived the 1980s/90s trend for assimilation or extermination by larger competitors. One such, until quite recently, was Blays of Twickenham, repairing and selling motorcycles, seen here above in 2006 at No. 199 Heath Road, on The Green side of The Dip, where Heath Road passes beneath the railway bridge. The larger houses on either side (No. 197 Heath Road on the left, Nos 1 and 3 The Green on the right) all appear on the 1863 OS map, but the protruding commercial unit (actually built on the wider angle of No. 197's front garden) probably dates from the early twentieth century. There was a strong family connection with Blays on my mother's side, as one of my uncles, George Anderson, and my cousin, Robert Anderson, worked here. Within a few years of the above photograph this shop was closed, and the last remaining shop, on the north side of The Green, followed a few years ago, around 2008.

This and next page: Three views, all taken in 2006, of the property on the corner of The Green (No. 64, listed in the 1939 *Kelly's Directory* as a baker's, although on the much older 1863 OS map it is marked as being the post office). The rear of No. 64 stretches away along May Road. There are two distinct sides to The Green. On the south side, still dominated by the Holy Trinity church (built 1841), are mostly large detached or semi-detached houses and leafy streets stretching away towards Strawberry Hill station (itself built about 1872). To the immediate west and north were more working-class terrace houses and cottages, pubs, breweries and other small industries, many – like Blays – motor repair or engineering. On the 1863 OS map May Road was called 'Chamberlain Road', and Colne Road was 'Back Road', being (until the 1890s) the limit of development, with allotments and orchards between it and the River Crane or the Windsor railway line. Knowle Road was called 'Harris Road', with empty space westward as far as the cut-way to Albion Road. By the 1894–96 OS map houses had appeared along Mereway Road, to be followed not long after by the development of Gould, Gravel and Andover Roads. Norcutt, Warwick and Hamilton Roads were built in the early 1900s.

Twickenham Green (known simply as The Green) is all that is left of the former Twickenham Common, itself the south-east extremity of the once extensive Hounslow Heath (hence Heath Road, from King Street to The Dip). In 1818, under the Enclosure Award, the 182 acres between Hanworth Road (modern-day Staines Road) and Hampton Road were divided up and sold off, giving birth to a number of new roads. These were originally called Workhouse Road, Middle Road, Third Common Road, Second Common Road and First Common Road – now First Cross through to Fifth Cross Roads respectively. The oldest properties in First Cross Road date from the early nineteenth century, mostly artisan cottages, while around 4 acres of the land across the road immediately facing them was originally given over to allotments. Only later, in the second half of the nineteenth century, did they revert back to the public domain. Above and below, Nos 11–15 viewed in the 1970s and again in 2007; comparatively little changed except for intrusive motor cars.

Above is another view of First Cross Road, showing Nos 4–10 as they appeared in the 1970s. Below is the almost rural view, perhaps taken about the same time, certainly still in the mid-1970s, of the corresponding rear gardens. I presume now that I gained access through one of the pedestrian cut-ways accessed from Second Cross Road.

Above: The same view of Nos 4–10 First Cross Road from The Green as seen in 2006. Unfortunately this is also a glaring example of how *not* to renovate an older property. Even in the earlier photograph the windows to Nos 4, 6 and 8 were already inappropriate to the period wooden sash windows, as seen still surviving in No. 10. But, thirty years later, this mismatch is further compounded by quite unsuitable 'mock Georgian' porches and the fake 'Dickensian Christmas card' window panes now installed in Nos 4 and 6; the latter also putting in smaller, square upstairs windows rather than former rectangular ones, made more obvious by the use of lighter yellow, rather than brown, brick. Oh, dear.

Opposite: Nos 16–19 First Cross Road, seen above in the 1970s, and again comparatively unchanged apart from the garden fencing in 2006. On the 1894–96 OS map the large red-brick building is marked as 'Church Institute' and, looking back to the 1863 map, had apparently replaced several smaller cottages previously occupying this site. Workhouse Road, the original name for First Cross Road, was named after the late eighteenth-century workhouse (demolished 1845) which once stood just to the north, on the other side of the Hanworth (now Staines) Road.

Above: Carpenters Court, on the south side of Hampton Road between Walpole Road and Wellesley Road, immediately opposite Third Cross Road, can be seen here in 2006. Although built early in the 1950s, the rather elegant modernist style is perhaps more reminiscent of the 1930s. Formerly this was the site of the Carpenter's Company almshouses, which were built in 1841 on 8 acres of land acquired a year earlier. They were eventually sold to Twickenham Council in 1947 and demolished in 1951.

Opposite: Two views of the front and side of Nos 114–18 Hampton Road: the first taken in the 1970s, the other in 2006 of the stepped side-entrance to No. 114, with what was probably a small outhouse or stables seen on the right (a building appears on 1863 OS map, but is already a separate unit by 1894). Although built after 1840 as part of a unified development by a Mr William Horsley, which includes Nos 120–34 Hampton Road and the twelve houses (originally thirteen) in Trafalgar Road, the specific style here, with wrought-iron building and stucco rendering, is more reminiscent of the Regency period. All were occupied by 1855, the six properties east of Trafalgar Road being designated as 'Prospect Villas' on the 1863 OS map, with the terrace of five houses between Trafalgar and Fourth Cross Roads being called 'Nelson Terrace'. Trafalgar Road itself was originally called 'Trafalgar Square', having two separate roads with a pond and greensward in the middle, but this was built over in 1882 by a single road, greatly enlarging the front gardens. To the north, Gothic Road was built around fifteen years later, with the breakup of the Gothic House estate between Fourth and Third Cross Roads. Even as long ago as 1969 it was recommended that this entire estate be made into a conservation area, with Grade II listings and protection of trees.

A 1970s view of Fourth Cross Road (*inset*), looking towards the junction with Denmark Road, with the old stables at the rear of the Prince of Wales public house (No. 136 Hampton Road, dating from 1841) in the near foreground. In the 1939 *Kelly's Directory* the shop still seen here in this earlier photograph was listed as a grocer's. In the larger 2012 picture all trace of the shop has completely vanished. The corner building is residential only, with the front entrance in Denmark Road, and the entire Fourth Cross Road ground-floor wall is bricked up and plastered over. Glimpsed in the right-hand distance of the later picture is The Rifleman public house, located on the corner of Bedford Road, which dates from 1870.

No. 175 Hampton Road, with beyond on the left what had formerly been the junction with Stanley Road, now blocked off to traffic to and from Teddington, which now diverts down the South Road dual carriageway. For many years this was The Nelson public house, the first publican being as long ago as 1837. It is now the Loch Fyne seafood restaurant.

Inset: This is the oldest of my photographs, taken around 1961–62, of me (still as a schoolboy) in the long front garden of my maternal grandmother's cottage at No. 6 South Road, then one of a parade of twelve semi-detached cottages formerly known as Prospect Place, set back from the road immediately down from what was then the Jolly Blacksmith public house. The original 1850s pub was demolished and rebuilt in 1932; it is now a Brouge bistro, renamed The Old Goat, specialising in Belgian-influenced cuisine. Those cottages can be seen on the 1863 OS map (predating the houses in Grove Road behind), but the bricked-up upstairs windows possibly indicate they may predate even the old pub. A few years after this picture, still in the 1960s, all the cottages to the right of my grandmother's were demolished and replaced by rather bland 'town houses' (Nos 7–13) with garages on the ground floor. Sadly, as already observed elsewhere, the desire for privacy has meant the surviving cottages, including this one, are now completely screened by shrubbery and fencing.

Above: Even at the time of the previous photograph South Road was already a short dual carriageway from the fire station to the junction of Sixth Cross Road, a comparative rarity which I remember rather confused the older motorist! Again looking at the 1863 OS map, and beyond what are now the half dozen townhouses where the last six cottages of Prospect Place once were, but set nearer to the road, were another dozen large houses, this time with long rear gardens. As this 2012 photograph of No. 20 South Road shows, they, at least, are still there, and many – like this wonderful example – are well-maintained and preserving period detail. The inscription on the façade reads, 'Valentine Cottages – E. D. G. – 1840.' The initials are probably these of the builder. The current owner informed me that the land was owned by the Duke of Northumberland (of Syon House), and in the deeds there is a covenant that, 'any gold or items of value found must be handed over the Northumberland Estate'.

Opposite: Two views of Fulwell railway station, taken in 2006: the first, from the still unsurfaced Wellington Gardens, of the main station building; and the second from the passenger footbridge actually over the railway line, again back towards the station building. What is now the Shepperton line reached Hampton in 1863 and this station was originally named Fulwell & Hampton Hill station. The line here was in a cutting which extends beneath Wellington Road Bridge, parallel to Hampton Hill High Street, and almost to Hampton station itself. For quite some time after this trains could only run from the direction of Twickenham, but later the additional rail link between the Strawberry Hill railway sheds and Teddington Cemetery was finally opened in 1901 to passengers coming from the Teddington and Kingston direction. Originally, before the construction of Fulwell tramway depot in 1902 (since 1935 used by buses only, the sheds of which can be seen on the right in the second picture), the station stood in splendid isolation, actually some distance from the centres of population it was meant to serve. However, even by the 1930s, major development had filled in most of the open land to the south between Wellington Road and Teddington Cemetery. The building obviously dates from the 1860s, and I can remember, even 100 years later, the external bracket lighting still being gas lit.

Acknowledgements

I would like to thank members of the Borough of Twickenham Local History Society (BOTLHS) for their help, especially Ken Howe, Kenneth Lea and Mike Cherry, for their contributions and assistance in my research concerning Teddington and Twickenham. Also, as always, Jane Baxter and her team at the Local Studies Library at the Old Town Hall, Richmond – always a wonderful source of local history, which I would recommend to anyone interested in the Borough of Richmond. I would also, belatedly, like to thank June Sampson, from the *Surrey Comet*, and Emma Rummins, of the Kingston upon Thames Local History Room, for their contributions and help when I was first tentatively researching my 1970s Kingston photographs as long ago as 2007. I would like to thank the staff at the Twickenham Museum for their help and interest in this project. I was able to access a number of excellent internet sources, including that of the excellent Twickenham Museum archives website and the Hampton Wick Society website. I would especially recommend Richard F. Holmes's local publication *Pubs, Inns and Taverns of Kingston*, by Wildhern Press, which I found very useful in the Kingston upon Thames section.

I also made reference to several previous publications from my own library collection, including the 1996 *Britain in Old Photographs: Twickenham, Teddington & Hampton* by Mike Cherry, Ken Howe and John Sheaf, which is still in print; the earlier *Twickenham as it Was* (published 1975) by the Borough of Twickenham Local History Society, and *Teddington as it Was* (published 1980) by the Teddington Society. Also the Teddington Society and P. A. Ching's *The Houses in Teddington, 1800 to 2000 AD* (published 1999), which again I would recommend. In the Local Studies Library archives I found the old pre-1970s *Kelly's Street Directories* to be a fascination source of useful local information, as well as their large-scale 1933 and 1863 Ordnance Survey maps. I would also recommend the excellent Alan Godfrey Maps reproductions of the Ordnance Survey maps for all of this area, the oldest being 1894 up to 1934.

Finally I would like to thank those individuals whose properties I photographed and who subsequently supplied me with useful information in South Road, Twickenham, and in Richmond Road, and especially Burleigh House, Broom Road, Teddington.

All photographs were taken by, or are the property of, the author. All opinions and comments expressed, and any unintentional errors within the text, are entirely those of the author.